On the Hay

Words to practise

hay day way

play stay away

sways

The lambs go to
play on the hay.

The lambs jump this way.

The lambs jump that way.

The lambs hop and skip on the hay all day.

Oh no! The hay will not stay still. It sways.

The hay sways this way and that way.

Bump! Bang!
Crash! The lambs
run away.